KU-728-190

page 5

page 25

Cool Cars

by
David Orme

Rans∞m

Thunderbolts

Cool Cars

by David Orme

Illustrated by Dylan Gibson

Published by Ransom Publishing Ltd.
Radley House, 8 St. Cross Road, Winchester, Hants. SO23 9HX, UK
www.ransom.co.uk

ISBN   978 178127 061 5

First published in 2013

Copyright © 2013 Ransom Publishing Ltd.

Illustrations copyright © 2013 Dylan Gibson

'Get the Facts' section - images copyright: cover, prelims, passim – Maciej Noskowski, Matěj Baťha, M 93; pp 6/7 - Martin Durrschnabel; pp 8/9 - Marc Ryckaert (MJJR), Brian Snelson, jaqian, Brian Hillegas; pp 10/11 - Ben Sutherland, David Hunt; pp 12/13 - Lothar Spurzem, Brian Snelson, M 93, aaron.bihari, Nevit Dilmen; pp 14/15 - Patrick Hutter, Schneelocke, Bill Philpot; pp 16/17 - Francesco Crippa, 36clicks, Morio, Nic Redhead; pp 18/19 - Kyu Oh, Christopher Batt, Maindru Photo; pp 20/21 - dbking, Dontworry, Dash; pp 22/23 - fotoVoyager, Cherubino, Brendan Hunter, Nuon Hans-Peter van Velthoven; p 36 - Francesco Crippa.

A CIP catalogue record of this book is available from the British Library.

Cool Cars: The Facts

127 mph   1906

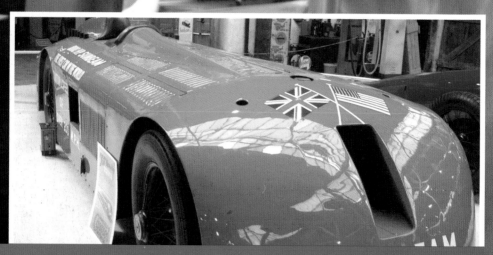

204 mph   1927

231 mph   1929

763 mph   1997

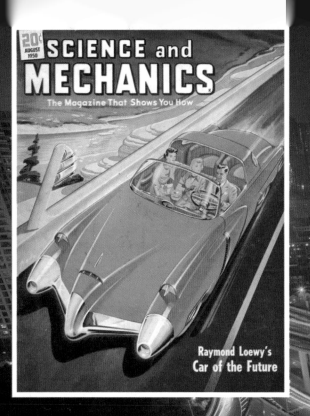

20¢
AUGUST
1950

SCIENCE and MECHANICS

The Magazine That Shows You How

Raymond Loewy's
Car of the Future

Need for Speed

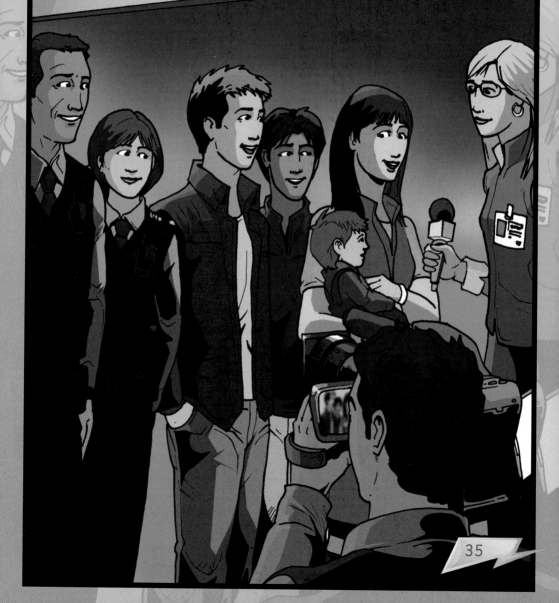

35